PRAYERPATH

PRAYERPATH
JACK HAYFORD

Tyndale House Publishers, Inc.
Wheaton, Illinois

All Bible quotations are taken from *The Living Bible,* copyright 1971 by Tyndale House Publishers, Wheaton, Illinois, unless indicated as being from *The Holy Bible,* New King James Version (NKJV), copyright 1979, 1980, 1982 by Thomas Nelson, Inc., Nashville, Tennessee, or *The Holy Bible,* King James Version (KJV).

This book was originally published under the title *Stepping up in Faith,* by Living Way Ministries, Van Nuys, California.

Library of Congress Catalog Card Number 86-51612
ISBN 0-8423-4964-2
Copyright 1984 by Jack Hayford
All rights reserved
Printed in the United States of America

95 94 93 92 91 90

11 10 9 8 7 6 5

Dedicated to my mama,
Dolores Hayford,
who has lived a life
of faithful prayer
and taught me to
do the same.

CONTENTS

Introduction 9

STEP ONE:
Confident Faith 13

STEP TWO:
Transforming Faith 19

STEP THREE:
Responsible Faith 25

STEP FOUR:
Dependent Faith 31

STEP FIVE:
Releasing Faith 35

STEP SIX:
Obedient Faith 43

STEP SEVEN:
Trusting Faith 49

INTRODUCTION

There is a call across America for believers to join in united prayer. This concept of a "prayer concert," of people praying together in the unity of the Holy Spirit, carries some refreshing prospects. And I hope that this booklet will serve to encourage, teach, and foster effective united prayer among the whole body of Christ.

"Prayer concerts" were first proposed in the United States during the eighteenth century by Jonathan Edwards, the man God used to spark the Great Awakening. Today we live in anticipation of yet another spiritual awakening—a global one—and concerted prayer is still the key.

God's Word gives us clear guidance into the reasons and purposes of concerted prayer: "If two of you agree down here on earth concerning anything you ask for, my Father in heaven will do it for you. For where two or three gather together because they are mine, I will be right there among them" (Matthew 18:19, 20). When we join together to pray in the love and faith of Jesus Christ it is more than an exercise in speculation or acting on a hope that something may happen. It is an act of deep belief that the harmony of our hearts, joined before the throne of God, will bring to fulfillment God's promises of revelation and power. And this agreeing of hearts joined in faith and prayer is exactly what Christ wanted to lead us toward when he taught what is generally referred to as the Lord's Prayer. Here is the prayer as recorded in Matthew 6:9-13:

> Pray ye: Our Father which art in heaven, Hallowed be thy name. Thy kingdom come. Thy will be done in earth, as it is in heaven. Give us this day our daily bread. And forgive us our debts, as we forgive our debtors. And lead us not into temptation, but deliver us from evil: For thine is the kingdom, and the power, and the glory, for ever. Amen. (KJV)

As familiar as these words are to nearly everyone, few of us really understand them as Christ intended them to be understood. He didn't teach this prayer just to be memorized or simply for the sake of recitation—yet that seems to be its general use and application today.

Of course, I'm not suggesting that we should

Introduction

stop reciting the Lord's Prayer, but I *am* suggesting that we need to study it and learn to apply its truths. We need to recognize that it is a pattern for prayer, an outline and introduction to the components of effective praying. In this teaching, Jesus lays seven foundational building blocks that, if utilized, can bring us to a place of trusting, restful confidence in prayer.

All seven of these building blocks or steps teach us about warm, vital praying and about effective, dynamic faith. Understanding these seven steps can change us into people of fruit-bearing faith, and can bring us closer together as people whose hearts are harmonized through agreement in prayer.

So join me in examining each of these building blocks, these steps to effective prayer. From the beginning truth of *relationship* shown in the first words of the prayer, to the concluding "thine is the kingdom, and the power, and the glory," Christ will lead us to a settled, secure confidence in God's ultimate triumph in our lives and our world.

Let our prayers produce a concert—a beautiful unity of spirit, in accordance with God's will and open to his power and fulfilled promises.

STEP ONE: CONFIDENT FAITH

"OUR FATHER WHICH ART IN HEAVEN..."
Jesus opens his teaching with an emphasis on our relationship with God as "Father." In doing so, he lays the foundational truth that we are given grounds for confidence in prayer on the strength of that "Father-child" relationship, which the Bible says is established and secured through Christ.

> And we are sure of this, that he will listen to us whenever we ask him for anything in line with his will. And if we really know he is listening when we talk to him and make our requests, then we can be sure that he will answer us. (1 John 5:14, 15)

There is nothing more crippling to effective prayer than not having confidence in our relationship with God. When Jesus refers to God as the "Father," he helps us to understand the glorious relationship we are intended to have with him.

Unfortunately, the concept of "father" has been marred for many through disappointing earthly relationships with parents or authority figures. Because of this common human fact, Jesus made a point to show us the Father in a way no one else ever could. For in Christ himself we see that God is a Father who transcends even the finest earthly father; he is able to redeem us from the broken images or painful memories of our lives. As we follow Christ's teachings about the Father and see him show us the Father in his life, we come to understand the power of his words to Philip: "Anyone who has seen me has seen the Father!" (John 14:9).

In Luke 15, Jesus uses the story of the prodigal son to paint a magnificent picture of what our Father God is really like.

Here is a young man who wasted everything he'd been given—his inheritance, his opportunities, and his father's trust. He ended up working in a pigpen. But in unfolding this story, Jesus unveils God's heart toward each of us through five essential phrases. He shows that, regardless of what we have wasted, God's arms are still reaching toward us, openly and lovingly.

The first thing we learn about is *God's quest for us.* We see this in the phrase that says the father saw the prodigal son when he was still "a long distance away" (v. 20). This shows us something unique and precious about the longing heart of God. For, as the father watched for his wayward son, so God's heart yearns and watches for each of us, even when we are far away from him. In other words, regardless of what we have done or where we are, *God loves us*.

Second, we see that when the father saw the son on his way home, he "was filled with loving pity and ran and embraced him and kissed him" (v. 20); he *received* his son.

I have often reflected on this story, thinking about the reluctance that son must have felt as he drew closer and closer to home. He must have been uneasy about his return, feeling very unworthy. He knew he had squandered his resources, had wasted his entire inheritance, and had nearly lost his life! He had every reason to doubt his father's acceptance.

But Jesus describes God's open heart toward us by showing how the young man's father welcomed him. The verb tense used here to say, "he embraced him and kissed him" literally translates "he kissed him repeatedly." The father must have received his wandering son with much the same joy that he'd had when he first embraced him at his birth. It was as though a brand new son was being born all over again! "This son of mine was dead and has returned to life. He was lost and is found!" (v. 24). And in this same way, it is with joy that *God receives us*.

Third, after this loving reception the father called for "the finest robe" to be given to his son.

The particular style of robe referred to was full-length in cut; in those days, a garment reserved only for those who held a position of honor and prestige. So it is clear that this fallen son was being *restored* to his former position as an heir in the household. The privileges of relationship with his father were returned to him, even though he had lost the inheritance he'd been given. Likewise, God not only *receives* us as forgiven sons, but he *restores* us from the loss our past has caused us. Although we may have abandoned the life-gifts he first gave us, he welcomes us back with a loving embrace and brings us again to our intended place in his will and purposes.

Fourth, the father had a "jeweled ring" put on his son's finger. How the hearts of those listening to this story for the first time must have leapt when Jesus related this part! They would have recognized instantly the significance of this action, for in ancient times the giving of such a ring indicated the son's full return to partnership with his father in the family's business. The ring gave him the right to exercise authority in all commercial or legal matters, for it represented the full weight of whatever authority or power that family name carried.

Thus, in calling us to pray "Our Father," Jesus has shown us how God invites us to let him *authorize us as his partner.* Our prayer in the "family name" of Jesus is authoritative prayer. And that name is given to us freely and fully, carrying with it all the rights and privileges granted to us as members of God's eternal family.

Fifth, the father had shoes or sandals placed on his son's feet. These shoes were more than mere clothing. Old Testament imagery teaches that people in mourning or grief commonly removed their shoes as a symbol of their sorrow. By placing shoes on his son's feet, the father was making an announcement to his son: "The time of mourning and the days of separation are over! The time of rejoicing has come!" And in this we see the final teaching of God's heart toward us: *God rejoices over us!* He rejoices at our return, and at the restored relationship we share with him.

Through the story of the prodigal son, Jesus illustrates our standing before God: We are welcomed to a place of confidence through the forgiveness given to us through Christ. Our Father offers us an authoritative right to be sons (John 1:12), to function in partnership with him and extend his dominion over all the earth. No matter what we fight, whether the powers of hell or our own weaknesses, eventual victory will be ours.

This is what Jesus wants to teach us when he instructs us to pray, "Our Father which art in heaven." He is founding all prayer on a growing relationship with a loving God. And as the truth of God's reception and our restoration fills us, we will discover yet another benefit: *We will learn to receive each other.* We begin, with

Christ's help, to see one another as brothers and sisters who have been received by a loving Father. And in that light, we can join together in harmony, lifting up a concert of powerful, effective prayer as people who have discovered God's love and are learning to pray confidently in him.

STEP TWO: TRANSFORMING FAITH

"HALLOWED BE THY NAME."
In the words, "Hallowed [holy] be thy name," we see the transforming power of prayer as Jesus introduces us to life's mightiest action: Worship. "Holy be your name" is a call to *worship* at the throne of God.

It helps to understand worship when we realize that the throne of God is an actual place. We are not just offering our worship "up there somewhere." In Revelation 4, John describes his glorious vision of God's throne and the mighty angelic beings around it. An innumerable host is seen worshiping God, saying, "Holy, holy, holy, Lord God Almighty—the one who was, and is, and is to come" (v. 8).

It is to this place that Jesus invites us, not just in an imaginary sense but in a living, dynamic sense of true worship. We are called to gather before our Father and to bring him our own offerings of praise.

Psalm 22:3 helps explain why worship is so important. It teaches that the worship of God's people literally makes a place for him to be enthroned in their midst:

> For thou art holy, O Lord; You who are enthroned upon the praises of Israel, your people. (Author's paraphrase)

Through this, we learn the dynamic objective of worship: it is God's way to bring his presence and power to his people. In other words, just as *we* enter into God's presence with worship, so *he* responds by coming into our presence. Our worship invites him to rule in our midst. And when our hearts are opened wide in worship, God will respond. His presence and power will come to change us and our circumstances.

So we can see the dual objective of worship: (1) To declare God's almighty greatness, and (2) To receive his power in our lives, situations, and needs.

In a dynamic sense, the words "Holy be thy name" are both an exalting of God and a humbling of ourselves. When we use those words, we are inviting the Holy Spirit to make God's presence and person real in our midst. Such encounters on a regular basis can only bring transformation—the conforming of our wills to God's, the shaping of our lives into his likeness.

> But we Christians have no veil over our faces; we can be mirrors that brightly reflect the glory of the Lord. And as the Spirit of the Lord works within us, we become more and more like him. (2 Corinthians 3:18)

Worship is not the only means to this transformation—we need to respond to the Word, obey the Holy Spirit, and walk in obedience daily—but worship *can* bring it about faster. To better understand transformation through worshiping, let's first examine the meaning of holiness, since that is the trait of God's nature that Jesus focuses on in this section of the Lord's prayer.

"Holy" is the worship expression heard most often around God's throne. But as often as it is said, both in heaven and here on earth, it is seldom understood. Too often, we consider holiness to be an external characteristic, a meditative expression, an organ-like speaking tone, a certain style of garments. The problem with this view is that we end up feeling intimidated or disqualified because we don't have the needed external traits of holiness.

On the other hand, some consider holiness to be a stern, forbidding trait of God's nature, a sort of attitudinal barrier on God's part—an obstacle created by his flaunting his perfection in the face of our weaknesses and sin. This, too, is wrong.

Simply stated, holiness is shown in the Bible as something relating to God's completeness. That is, God's holiness essentially acknowledges that he is complete; there is nothing lacking in his person, and nothing needs to be added to make him "enough." God's holiness also holds a promise: Because his holiness is complete, and because it is God's nature to give, he wants to share his holiness with us to complete us. He is ready to pour himself into us, to complete those areas of our lives that are lacking or "unholy" because of our sin.

As we open ourselves through worship to this desire of God's, we will find his holiness and wholeness overtaking our *un*holiness. His presence, responding to our worship, will begin to sweep away whatever residue remains from the destruction caused by our past sins.

In worship-filled prayer, a spiritual genetic begins to take effect. The traits and characteristics "born" into us when we became a part of God's family will begin to grow, making us more and more like him. Just as surely as physical traits are transmitted to us by our earthly parents, so the nature and likeness of our heavenly Father will grow in us as we learn and grow more in worshiping him.

This truth is reflected in the command, "You must be holy, for I am holy" (Leviticus 11:45; 1 Peter 1:16). Those verses hold a promise of holiness and completeness. They are not so

Transforming Faith

much a demand that we stretch ourselves through self-produced devices of "holiness" as they are God's guarantee that his life in us will become increasingly evident and powerfully transforming. Jesus calls us into the Father's presence to give the Father the opportunity to remake us in his likeness.

That's transformation!—a transformation that allows God to extend his kingdom through us. And this personal dimension of transformation is only the beginning.

Beyond the power of worship-filled prayer to change *us*, we can also achieve a wider area of impact on *others*. As God changes us his holiness is projected beyond us through prayer-power, and we will find that our prayers are changing other people and situations. In instructing us to enter the Father's presence with worship, Jesus points the way to a faith that can transform all of our lives and the lives of those we encounter. He says, "Since God is your Father, let your worship in his presence make you more like him; and as you do, his working in you will affect those around you."

So let us enter his presence with worship! Let's take the faith-step that moves us to experience the transforming power of God's rule in our lives and character, and through our faithful prayers.

STEP THREE: RESPONSIBLE FAITH

"THY KINGDOM COME. THY WILL BE DONE IN EARTH, AS IT IS IN HEAVEN." This section of the Lord's Prayer shows us how Christ intended us to effectively discharge our *responsibility* in prayer. His counsel on how to pray illuminates a truth that we often ignore: Man needs to invite God's rule and power into the affairs of this life through prayer. If mankind won't pray, God's rule is forfeited.

That thought runs against the common supposition, "If God wants to do something, he'll just *do* it." This sorry strain of fatalism infests many minds. But the idea of man as a pawn moved by the Almighty at his whim is totally removed from the truth revealed in Scripture. Jesus shows us that man is responsible for inviting God's rule—his benevolent purpose, presence, and power—into this world. Rather than demonstrating man as a hopeless, helpless victim of circumstance, the Bible declares that *redeemed* man is hopeful and capable of expecting victory when he prays in faith. The grounds for this understanding can be found in the beginning of the Bible.

Man's Loss. In Genesis 1, the Bible states that dominion over this planet was given to man. That assignment was not only one of privilege, but one of making man responsible for what happens here (Genesis 1:28). Unless we understand this fact, we will never really understand that most of the confusion, agony, and distress in our world exists as a direct result of our having betrayed God's trust. As a race, we violated the responsibility God gave us.

This betrayal began at the fall of man. Through that tragedy we have suffered inestimable loss. Man not only lost his relationship with God, but he lost his ability to rule responsibly as well. His authority to extend God's rule over the earth is completely frustrated—whether the issue is nuclear arms or managing the children at home.

And now, according to the Bible, "All the rest of the world around us is under Satan's power and control" (1 John 5:19). So man's fall betrayed the God-given trust of ruling Earth into the hands of the devil, Satan, the "Evil One." Since the Fall, mankind has not only been vulnerable to satanic deceptions, but by our own sin and rebellion we have contributed to the confused mess our world has become. Between man's sinning and Satan's hateful quest to destroy, death and destruction have invaded every part of life as we know it—breaking relationships, dashing hopes and dreams, and ruining destinies.

God's Restoration. But when our betrayal of God's trust turned this world over to the powers of death, God lovingly provided us with another option—a living option in the person of his Son. God sent Jesus, whose ministry announced the possibility of man's restoration to God's kingdom: "Turn from sin, and turn to God, for the Kingdom of Heaven is near" (Matthew 4:17). In that statement, Jesus made it clear that the rule of God was once again being made available to man. No longer did mankind need to remain a hopeless victim of sin and hell!

In his ministry, both then and now, Jesus manifests every aspect of the kingdom he offers. When Jesus heals, he is showing what can happen when the rule of God enters a situation. When he answers need at any dimension, he is putting into action the power of God's rule available for our lives. As Jesus teaches, his objective has always been to help straighten out our thinking about what God is like, so that we might respond correctly to him and his kingdom.

But at the same time that Jesus ministers, hell seeks to level its hostile devices against the

King and kingdom he offers. Consequently, Jesus demonstrates a warlike *opposition* to the invisible powers of darkness. He is well-known for demonstrating God's love; but he is equally well-known for the way he confronts the demonic powers of hell. In the climactic act of his crucifixion he smashed these powers, making possible the offer of reentry into divine life with God and paving the way for us, his followers, to also strike down any of the satanic powers we encounter (Mark 16:17-20; Colossians 2:15).

Man's Responsibility. In light of these truths, mankind must decide whether or not they will draw on the resources of Christ's triumph through the cross and advance God's kingdom. Acceptance of Christ *begins* our participation in this kingdom (John 3:3, 5), and we are then called to *advance* it, sharing the gospel of Christ with the world around us (Matthew 24:14; Acts 1:8). And there is no more effective way to accelerate this advance than for believers to pray together! Our first steps in faith are made on the feet of prayer, whether we are moving into victory or into witness. Recognize that faith and victory are *not* achieved through the zeal of human excitement, but by prayer that acknowledges Calvary's triumph as a release for God's presence and power.

This is what Jesus' instructions to pray "Thy kingdom come" reveal to us. By such prayer we are taking on our role as members of a race who once betrayed the King, but who now welcome his entry into every need and pain of this planet. The power is God's, but the privilege *and* responsibility to pray are ours. So let us come together at his throne, expecting and receiving the flow of the Holy Spirit's power, by whose anointing we will be able to witness God's purposes being accomplished through us.

We must see the rule and power of the Kingdom of God as present, practical, and personal possibilities in every dimension of our daily lives. We must not let the promise of the future kingdom keep us from possessing the dimensions of victory that God has for us *now*. And the fact that Jesus is coming again to establish his kingdom over all the earth should not cause us to neglect our present responsibilities for advancing the gospel. Until he comes again, Jesus directed us to "occupy" (Luke 19:13). That "occupation" entails drawing on the resources of God's kingdom and power, reaching into the realm of the invisible through prayer, and changing one circumstance after another.

"Thy kingdom come. Thy will be done on earth, as it is in heaven." It is our privilege to pray this. And our responsibility.

STEP FOUR: DEPENDENT FAITH

"GIVE US THIS DAY OUR DAILY BREAD."
In this next phrase, Jesus is talking about more than just having enough food or having our physical needs met. He is issuing an invitation for us to come to the Father daily for refreshing, for renewal and nourishment for both our souls and our bodies. This phrase, "Give us this day our daily bread," registers a specific command for us to recognize our *dependency* on the Lord for *all* nourishment, and to realize that this provision for our needs flows out of the discipline of daily prayer.

James 4:2 makes a strong statement regarding the necessity of prayer: "The reason you don't have what you want is that you don't ask God for it." These words show that the Lord is ready to release many things to us—but we need to ask him for them. The promises or prophecies of God's care for us do not bypass our need for prayer. The Lord calls us to willingly turn to him and call in prayer for him to work in our lives. Rather than relying on our own strength (chin up, teeth clenched: "I'm going to get this done"), we need to come to the Father in prayer.

Dependent prayer is not desperate or demeaning prayer. It is neither frantic (as though we only resorted to turning to God in a crisis), nor depersonalizing (as though God required us to grovel in order to escape his wrath). In contrast to these distorted views, dependent prayer is both the way we gain a personal realization of God's unswerving commitment *to* us and how we participate in God's promised provision *for* us.

Psalm 90:12 says, "Teach us to number our days and recognize how few they are; help us to spend them as we should." We need to learn an accountability for each day's hours and events, and dependent prayer can help us do this. Jesus is not teaching us just to request "bread" at morning, noon, and night. He is teaching us to ask for the Father's direction and provision in every event and hour of our day.

Committing each day's details to God in prayer—requesting "today's bread"—can deliver you from pointless pursuits and wasted time. Such prayer paves the way to victorious days. "My times are in Your hands: deliver me from the hand of my enemies" (Psalm 31:15, NKJV). What wisdom! When you put your day in God's hands,

Dependent Faith

any enemy you face can be conquered. Whether your enemy is yourself—procrastination, sloth, or other weaknesses—or a demonic conspiracy that Satan has plotted against you, the Lord is able to deliver you. He can help you overcome anything that might wrench your life from his purpose, or cause valuable time to slip through your fingers.

Submit your day to the Lord and ask him to provide for your needs. Whether your need is food or counsel for the day's activities, you will find that it *will* be provided. He will faithfully respond when you set your time in his hands.

And when we learn to pray this way we will find another wonderful promise being fulfilled: "May your strength match the length of your days" (Deuteronomy 33:25). As we learn to pray, "Give us this day our daily bread," we will find in the Lord a strength proportionate to each day's needs. Whatever challenges a day holds—confrontations, difficulties, even tragedy—we will receive the strength to face it. Just as we derive physical strength and nourishment from eating daily bread, so we will gain spiritual strength and nourishment when we learn the wisdom of acknowledging our dependency upon the Father, and pray his way.

STEP FIVE: RELEASING FAITH

"FORGIVE US OUR DEBTS, AS WE FORGIVE OUR DEBTORS."

The next point in the Lord's prayer addresses our need for forgiveness. Some people use the word "trespasses" and others use the word "debts" for this section of the prayer. Both expressions are accurate and uniquely significant. In fact, we need to pray *both* ways, for in these two expressions Jesus shows us the two sides of human disobedience: sins of *commission* and sins of *omission*, wrong things we have done and right things we neglected to do.

"Forgive us our trespasses" speaks to our need to ask the Lord to forgive us for having "stepped over the line." God is concerned about trespassing because he wants to keep us from the things that will damage or destroy us. In his Word he set certain guidelines—territorial boundaries, if you will—that say, "Do not trespass here." When we violate these commands, we are guilty of a sin of commission.

"Forgive us our debts" relates to our failures, where it might be said that we "owed it" to the situation to do differently than we did. In failing to act rightly, we become debtors. And such indebtedness can hang like a cloud over the soul, hindering our sense of freedom and faith for the future.

And so, with this phrase of asking forgiveness, Christ fashions into our regular pattern of prayer a request for release from the shame of guilt or the pain of neglect.

To grasp the power potential in this prayer for forgiveness, we need to see that both of the phrases are conditional. They are linked to the words "as we forgive." Jesus specifically states that the degree of our forgiveness, our willingness to release others, establishes a standard of measurement. He gives back to us the measurement of release and forgiveness that we show others. This brings us to the heart of life's most practical truth: If I do not move in God's dimension of release and forgiveness toward others, I will become an obstruction to my own life and growth.

Dual Dimensions. We need to see that "forgiving faith" has a dual dimension: (1) We must confess our own sinning; and (2) We must forgive others.

First, by emphasizing our need for forgiveness of sin, Jesus isn't shaking a stick of condemnation in our faces. That isn't the issue. The real problem is that we are all somewhat warped—people bent from God's original design and purpose. Not one of us is flawless, no one is without selfishness and pride. Sin is an inherited inclination in us all, and it needs to be forgiven.

Jesus taught us to pray for forgiveness on a regular basis not to remind us of our sinfulness but to keep us from becoming sloppy in our ideas about the grace of God. Too often, we distort God's grace and give in to the deception that "I can do anything I want as long as God's grace encompasses me." But in Romans 6:1, 2, the Word demands pointedly, "Well then, shall we keep on sinning so that God can keep on showing us more and more kindness and forgiveness? Of course not!" In calling us to pray "Forgive us our trespasses," Jesus isn't seeking to remind us of our failures, but he *does* want to sensitize us to sin, and to the fact that this sin hinders our growth in him.

God's forgiveness is graciously offered and abundantly available. He warmly invites us to pardon, cleansing, and release in the Scriptures:

> He has removed our sins as far away from us as the east is from the west. (Psalm 103:12)
>
> Once again you will have compassion on us. You will tread our sins beneath your

> feet; you will throw them into the depths of
> the ocean! (Micah 7:19)
>
> I will never again remember their sins
> and lawless deeds. (Hebrews 10:17)
>
> If we confess our sins to him, he can be
> depended on to forgive us and to cleanse us
> from every wrong. (1 John 1:9)

Forgiveness can be counted on. The condition—confession—is presented clearly, and the availability is promised: "He can be depended on to forgive us."

Second, Jesus describes forgiveness as being relayed *through* us to others:

> So if you are standing before the altar in
> the Temple, offering a sacrifice to God, and
> suddenly remember that a friend has something against you, leave your sacrifice there
> beside the altar and go . . . and be reconciled
> to him, and then come and offer your
> sacrifice to God. (Matthew 5:23, 24)
>
> But when you are praying, first forgive
> anyone you are holding a grudge against, so
> that your Father in heaven will forgive you
> your sins too. (Mark 11:25)

The Word expands and applies the truth that we who have received forgiveness need to be forgiving. Jesus directs us to go to anyone who has something against us and, in an attitude of humility and forgiveness, rectify our relationship

Releasing Faith

with him. And he says this must be done before we can make a serious, honest approach to him in worship.

When we go to another for reconciliation, we must be certain we are not doing so in an attempt to justify ourselves. If someone has a difference of opinion or some problem with me, regardless of whose fault it is, God will not allow me to make any charge against that person. Christ desires that we be willing to go the extra mile and assume the role of reconciler—just as he did for us in reconciling us to the Father.

Understanding that people often perceive a situation opposite of how it really is will help us to act as Christ commands. For example, if you have been offended, you may be completely unaware of the viewpoint of the one you feel has hurt you. To the other person, it usually seems as though *he* was the one violated, and you are at fault. The effects of sin and Satan's discord in our lives make us all terribly vulnerable to natural misunderstandings. We must acknowledge that in order to open up the reconciling process. When we become willing to go to others, to recognize that their attitudes toward us are based on something that they perceive as being our fault, and accept the burden of the misunderstanding (as Jesus did to bring peace between God and man), a release will be realized. If we accept the responsibility for whatever has breached our relationships with others, restored relationships can become possible.

Naturally, there may be times when the most loving, scriptural stand we can take is to confront others with their wrong. Jesus did that, and the Holy Spirit will show us when we are to do so. But the Spirit of forgiveness never does this in a self-defensive way; rather it operates in a spirit of reconciliation. This kingdom order of forgiveness will not always be easy. By nature we all prefer to be "in the driver's seat," so to speak. And the ministry of reconciling puts us at the mercy of the other person's response. But this is exactly where Jesus put himself when he laid down his life to offer forgiveness to all. Like him, we are not called to be someone's doormat, but we *are* called to learn his pathway to dominion. We must see that this kingdom path to power is in the Spirit of the Lamb, and not one of self-defense.

The Unforgiving Servant. Besides teaching us how we should pray, Jesus also says that prayer doesn't get far if it comes from a heart that consciously holds a bad attitude toward another person. The same applies if someone knowingly allows tension to exist between himself and someone else. Regardless of the details of a problem, we are called upon to *at least* make an effort to reconcile, and *always* to keep our hearts in a stance of forgiveness toward others.

Jesus elaborated on this truth in the parable of the unforgiving servant, found in Matthew 18:22-35. (It is important that you take a few minutes and read *all* of this parable. Please stop right now and do so.) Consider what Jesus was

Releasing Faith

saying. He told us of a forgiven servant who failed to show that same forgiveness to another. When Jesus described how the servant's master was angered by the ungraciousness of that servant, notice how he illustrated the consequences of unforgiveness: The unforgiving servant is delivered to the bill collectors until all he owes is paid in full.

This story demonstrates God's consistency. He has said, "If you don't forgive when you've been forgiven, you will find yourself confined and frustrated." He isn't saying you are lost again, but that the peace you first received when you opened your heart to God will sour and dissipate in a climate of unforgiveness. Invariably, the joy of the Lord departs when we refuse to mirror the acceptance and forgiveness he has shown to us.

Like the unforgiving servant, there are people who are tortured in mind and body, in relationships and circumstances. Often this is related to their being unwilling to forgive. This is why our forgiveness of others is such a vital step toward powerful prayer, because it releases in us, and to us, the full power of God's forgiveness.

There is no greater step upward in faith than the one we take when we learn to forgive, and do it. It blesses people who need our love and acceptance, and it releases us to bright horizons of joy, health, and dynamic faith in prayer.

STEP SIX:
OBEDIENT FAITH

"LEAD US NOT INTO TEMPTATION, BUT DELIVER US FROM EVIL."

Our sixth step brings us to the most paradoxical part of the Lord's Prayer: "Lead us not into temptation, but deliver us from evil." At first, these words seem confusing in light of other Scriptures which assure us that God does not tempt anyone. But passages such as James 1:13, 14 make it clear that Jesus is not teaching us that we have to beg God not to trick us into sinning. Nor is Jesus teaching us a prayer for escaping the demands of growth that come through God's leading us—and he *does* lead us—into trial.

To understand what Jesus *is* teaching we must first gain a clear understanding of the word "temptation," a word that carries a two-sided meaning. First, temptation essentially has to do with the desire of an adversary to test and break through our defenses. Second, temptation deals with the strength gained through encountering an adversary; that is, when the one who is tempted overcomes the tempter, the resulting victory builds strength. Temptation, therefore, is both positive and negative, depending on our viewpoint and response.

In that light, Jesus isn't suggesting that we should ask or expect to avoid the kind of confrontation he faced with Satan. In fact, the Bible tells us that the Holy Spirit *led* Christ into that experience of conflict with the devil (Matthew 4:1). As a direct result of overcoming this time of temptation, Jesus was brought to a place of victory and dominion over the Enemy (John 14:30). So this section of the Lord's Prayer holds a promise of victory, rather than a plea for relief from struggle.

We are not asking God not to play with us as pawns on a chessboard, risking our loss by "leading us" into a questionable situation. Rather, in examining various translations of this challenging verse and noting the tense and mood of the Greek verb *lead* or *bring into*, I have discovered that the phrase "Lead us not into temptation" is a guarantee of victory if we'll take it! Jesus is actually directing us to pray: "Father, should we at any point be led into temptation, we want to come out delivered and victorious."

So the issue in this portion of the Lord's Prayer is not God's character, but *ours*. Such praying is saying, "Lord, you won't lead or introduce me

Obedient Faith

into any situations but those for my refinement, growth, and victory. Therefore, when I encounter circumstances designed to lead me astray, I will recognize that it isn't your will for me to walk that way. And, by the words of this prayer, I commit myself in advance to *wanting* victory, to seeking deliverance, and to taking the way of escape you have promised me."

Here, then, is obedient faith confronting the reality of temptation and our vulnerability to it. Temptation is sometimes so quick in its rise and so subtle in its approach that we need to have established our steps in advance through regular prayer. We must come to the Lord and commit ourselves to receive his deliverance rather than allow temptation to entangle us in its snares. This prayer doesn't question God's nature or leading, but declares that we are casting ourselves on him.

Once again, it's important to understand the intent of this prayer because man is so easily deluded by temptation. Jesus is not suggesting that it is God's nature to seek our corruption through temptation, but that it is God's nature to "deliver us from evil." The prayer simply establishes a commitment on our part to receive the triumphant life Christ offers us in dominion over evil. Living becomes more effective when we avoid being neutralized by hell's manipulations or by our flesh's cry for self-indulgence.

Our Defense. The first line of defense against temptation that God gives us is listed in Ephesians 6:16: "The shield of faith," a part of the whole armor of God. This shield is easily raised. It happens whenever a person calls on the Lord: "Help me, Lord! The Enemy is attacking me!" The shield is available right now, so lift it when attacked. Take to heart the assurance of Joel 2:32, "Everyone who calls upon the name of the Lord shall be saved!"

God's Word promises us that the prayer Jesus taught has a guaranteed answer. First Corinthians 10:13 gives us these comforting words: "No temptation is irresistible. You can trust God to keep the temptation from becoming so strong that you can't stand up against it, for he has promised this and will do what he says. He will show you how to escape temptation's power so that you can bear up patiently against it."

Scripture tells us that the things that clutch at us are not unusual; everybody faces them. That doesn't remove temptation's challenge, but it does help us understand that we aren't evil simply because we're tempted. Furthermore, we have a certain promise: God has a doorway of exit for us! When temptation comes, the prayer "deliver us from evil" insures us a way out.

What a great certainty this is. What a beautiful climax to this lesson in the Lord's Prayer.

> Yes, and the Lord will always deliver me from all evil and will bring me into his heavenly Kingdom. To God be the glory

Obedient Faith

> forever and ever. Amen. (2 Timothy 4:18)
> So also the Lord can rescue you and me from the temptations that surround us. (2 Peter 2:9)

Scripture clearly teaches that God will deliver us out of temptation if we seek him. Thus, when we pray "deliver us from evil" we are committing ourselves to walking in triumph and dominion over the things that would seek to conquer us. We are living in obedient faith.

And when we live this way, we can count on God's deliverance, for "he is able!"

STEP SEVEN: TRUSTING FAITH

"FOR THINE IS THE KINGDOM, AND THE POWER, AND THE GLORY, FOR EVER. AMEN."
Our study of the Lord's Prayer is climaxed in examining these words of trusting faith: "For thine is the *kingdom,* and the *power,* and the *glory,* for ever." Here is the active expression of a heart that has found the absolute assurance of the complete triumph of God . . . in *his* time.

Acts 1:6, 7 gives us additional insight into this section of the Lord's Prayer:

> They asked him, "Lord, are you going to free Israel [from Rome] now and restore us as an independent nation?"
> "The Father sets those dates," he replied, "and they are not for you to know."

Jesus spoke these words following his resurrection, as final instructions to his men before his ascension. He had been explaining principles of the Kingdom of God, and the disciples had gotten confused (Acts 1:3-5). In light of what he was teaching, and with the facts of the crucifixion and the resurrection behind them, Jesus' disciples inquired: "Just when will this kingdom finally come?" They must have been sure, since Jesus continued to speak of the kingdom as he had before his death, that the time was ripe for the Messianic kingdom to be established. Surely now was the time for Israel to be liberated from Roman oppression.

But Jesus patiently replied that it wasn't for them to know when that would take place (v. 7). He wasn't stalling them, but redirecting their understanding. The issue of the kingdom's "coming with power" is asserted in the very next verse:

> But when the Holy Spirit has come upon you, you will receive power to testify about me with great effect, to the people in Jerusalem, throughout Judea, in Samaria, and to the ends of the earth. (Acts 1:8)

This conversation between Jesus and his disciples, with Jesus' promise of the Holy Spirit's power in relation to the timing of his kingdom, can help us understand the meaning of the concluding phrase of the Lord's Prayer. We can see that Jesus was teaching the pathway to *trust*—to the knowledge that when we have prayed in faith, we can rest firm in our confidence that God has heard.

Consider the words, "Thine is the kingdom." For many, these words seem to point to the future. But Jesus taught very clearly that the presence and power of the kingdom are given to us *now:* "So don't be afraid, little flock. For it gives your Father great happiness to give you the Kingdom" (Luke 12:32). Although we will experience the fullest expression of his kingdom when he comes again, we mustn't diminish the fact that this prayer is dealing with God's rule and power in our lives *now.* Wherever the Spirit is given room and allowed to work, the kingdom "comes."

But here, at prayer, Jesus is reminding us that such privileged participation in the power of his kingdom life has terms: We are called to submit to God's rule in our lives.

> Therefore submit to God. Resist the devil and he will flee from you. (James 4:7, NKJV)
> If you will humble yourselves under the mighty hand of God, in his good time he will lift you up. (1 Peter 5:6)

The Power and the Glory. The first factor in developing a trusting faith is learning that the rule, the power, and the glory *are* God's. He allows us to share with him, but he is Lord. He gives us power, but only he is omnipotent. He teaches us, but he alone is all-knowing. And the submitting and humbling spoken of in James and 1 Peter are prerequisites to sharing God's authority. Satan flees the believer who has learned the truth of *"thine* is the power."

Faith is ever and always challenging the status quo where evil reigns, pain and sickness prevail, hatred and hellishness rule, and human failure breeds confusion. As we learn to live under God's Holy Spirit's rule, we will be able to take a bold, confrontive stance against all in opposition to that rule—whether demon, flesh, or circumstance. Such a stance says, "I rely upon the One who claims ultimate and final rule everywhere. I won't give way to any lie that attempts to cast doubt on God's ultimate, complete victory." And when we do this, we often see results.

But what about when we don't see any results? What then? The disciples' inquiry echoes from our lips, too: "Will the kingdom be now?" To this question, Jesus teaches us to pray, "Thine is the kingdom." Even though it may not have fully appeared yet, two things come from trusting faith: (1) The knowledge that the ultimate triumph of God's manifest power shall come in his time; and (2) The assurance that, until that time, he has given us his Spirit to enable us to do his will.

Here is our fortress of confidence. Although time may pass without our always seeing "victory" as we would interpret it, we still have not been deserted. God's Holy Spirit brings us his

Trusting Faith

presence and power right now, for whatever circumstance we encounter.

While there are times when we will see God's kingdom power in action—in healings and miracles in our lives—there are also times that the Lord simply says, "Trust me—the time is not yet; but in the meantime the power of my Spirit will sustain you."

Great power and privilege *are* given to the Church. "Nothing will be impossible for you," Jesus says (Matthew 17:20, NKJV). Yet, as certain as the promise and possibilities are, we must acknowledge that there are times when we seem unable to possess this promise. Such an acknowledgement is not a statement of doubt, nor is it a case of God refusing to grant us an answer or fulfill his Word—God's promises are true and his Word is faithful—but the "kingdom timing" is his! And so are the ultimate power and glory.

So when we conclude the Lord's Prayer with, "Thine is the kingdom, and the power, and the glory," we aren't being either passive or poetic. We are reflecting the power of trusting faith: the faith that stands in firm confidence, regardless of circumstances. This faith declares, "Lord, to you belongs all kingdom authority, you are the possessor of all! And as I gain that kingdom, a portion at a time, I trust you—for the kingdom is yours."

There are no greater grounds for rest and contentment in life than the certainty wrapped in these words:

> "Thine is the kingdom"—all rule belongs to God.
> "Thine is the power"—all mightiness flows from him.
> "Thine is the glory"—his victory shall be complete.

With that kind of prayer comes boldness, confidence, and rest. For when all is said and done, our greatest resource is the resource of God's greatness. In this we can find confidence that our every need will be met, our ultimate victory realized, and that his time, purpose, and glory will prove to be the wisest, richest, and best.

Let us join the angelic throngs at his throne, uniting our concert of prayer and praise with theirs, saying, "Holy, holy, holy—Lord God *Almighty!*"

Other Resources

AUDIO CASSETTE TAPES
Related teachings by Jack Hayford are available through the SoundWord Tape Ministry. A complete catalog of tapes can be obtained by writing to: SoundWord Tape Ministry, 14300 Sherman Way, Van Nuys, CA 91405-2499.

VIDEOTAPES
Videotapes for use in homes, Bible studies, small group meetings, and churches may be special ordered. For information and a catalog of current listings, please write to: Living Way Ministries, 14300 Sherman Way, Van Nuys, CA 91405-2499.

Other Books by Jack Hayford

Along with *Prayerpath* there are several other booklets in this series by Jack Hayford available from Tyndale House Publishers.

Daybreak
A handbook on daily prayer that directs the reader to present all of his life and self to God. Jack Hayford discusses how believers can establish daily time with God, and he gives guidelines for preparing one's heart and day so that it becomes a daily habit to have a daybreak meeting with God.

Newborn
Expressly prepared for the new believer as a clear statement of exactly what Christ's salvation and one's new birth involve. A practical guide for learning to walk and live in the family of God. This book also includes a simple but profound section dealing with the meaning and dynamic of water baptism. While written to the new believer, it is designed so that even the most advanced will discover fuller dimensions of truth about their resources in Christ since their water baptism.

Spirit-Filled
Practical instruction on the person and power of the Spirit, teaching how, when, and where to put the spiritual gifts and graces to use in your life. Encourages the reader to open to the fullness of the Spirit of Christ and shows how to maintain wisdom and balance in daily Spirit-filled living.

The following book by Jack Hayford is also available from Tyndale House Publishers:

The Visitor
A study of the suffering of Christ that gives the reader an uncluttered insight into the reasons for and results of Christ's visit to mankind. A perceptive, on-target

treatment that enables readers to meet the Visitor face to face, recognizing his endless love and accepting his purpose and plan in their lives.